Rhona Whiteford

Acknowledgements

The author would like to thank the following people for their very kind co-operation, help and enthusiasm for the project:

St Oswald's Catholic Primary School, Headteacher Tony Brown, Literacy Governor Anne Ward, Reception class teachers Wendy Owen and Jane Hill;

St David Haigh and Aspull CE Primary School, Headteacher Julie Charnley, Reception class teacher Chris Charnock.

Sounds Shop (page 21)

First published in 2000 by BELAIR PUBLICATIONS LIMITED
Albert House, Apex Business Centre, Boscombe Road, Dunstable, Beds, LU5 4RL

© 2000 Belair on behalf of the author Rhona Whiteford

Editor: Elizabeth Miles   Design: Jane Conway   Photography: Roger Brown   Cover design: Martin Cross

'A Hive for a Honey Bee' from *This Little Puffin*, published by Puffin Books.
'A Dingle Dangle Scarecrow' from *This Little Puffin*, published by Puffin Books.
'Can't Catch Me' from *The Gingerbread Man*, published by Ladybird 1997, written by Ronnie Randall and illustrated by Terry Burton.

ISBN 0 94788 241 3

The cover photograph is taken from page 25, 'The Vowel Bunch'.

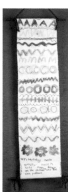

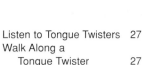

Contents

Introduction

We live in a communications-driven world which uses the spoken and written word as major tools, and the children in our care want to be a part of this. It is our job to provide a planned and balanced approach to developing the necessary skills. When learning is presented as interesting, useful and necessary, it will motivate and inspire.

The development of literacy relies on the acquisition of a range of skills which must grow together and feed off each other. If a child enjoys reading we know that a vital motivation trigger has been released, even though a child who loves reading may not necessarily enjoy writing, and could find spelling a problem at first.

This book has been written to provide ideas which can be used to motivate young children toward having an abiding interest in the very bones of literacy, the words and their spelling. Spelling can certainly be taught using a development spelling programme, but that vital enthusiasm for words is 'caught' from the teacher. The ideas, techniques and aids collected in this book are hopefully infectious – they have all been used enthusiastically by the young children I have taught.

Rhona Whiteford

Word Recognition

One of the most familiar words and one that children usually learn to recognise quickly is their first name. In order to celebrate the individual, to welcome the new children into school and introduce everyone, it is useful to begin the year with a project on names.

'Here we are!'

Begin by teaching the children to spell the word they will learn quickly – their name. This graph shows the children's first names in alphabetical order and is an excellent reference for learning names and for activities involving data, counting, numerical order and alphabetical order.

Take a photograph of each child holding a name card and check that the name cards can be read easily. Mount the photographs to create a graph as shown above. If possible, include the whole alphabet and leave blanks to show the existence of any letters that are not used, although this is not vital. Extend by adding lists of the names under each letter, copying the colour code to highlight the initial letter to aid a match for the children reading it.

Pets' Names

These displays will stimulate conversation about names and can also be used to start a topic on animals or for sorting activities in which, for example, they are put into sets according to size, colour of coat and the food they eat.

Ask the children to bring in photographs of their pets. Mount each photograph on a larger rectangle of different coloured card and write the pet's name underneath. Write a title for the display on card and cut it into the shape of a pet.

Name Poem

Display the following poem and surround it with coloured paper shapes on which the first names of all the children and helpers in the class are written. Self-portrait paintings by the children can also be added if desired.

My Name

My name is very special
And it belongs to me
I take it with me everywhere
But it's nothing you can see.

I write it on a paper
Or see it in my book.
And if I want to read it,
I use my eyes and look.

I spot the first big letter,
The shape of all my name.
I look at each bit carefully,
Then I'll know it once again.

Now I can write and read
   my name
I can also read much more,
That's the thing about this
   reading game ...
It opens up a door!

Giant Class List

Write a class list of the children's first names on a piece of white paper about 1 metre by 20 centimetres in size. Add the names of the teacher and assistants, too. Use a selection of coloured pens to help with recognition, for example a child may find it easier to remember that their name is 'the red one near the top'. The child will use colour as a clue before looking for other clues such as the first letter shape or word length. In teaching the children's names, encourage them to look at the whole word shape and, later, the initial letter.

Write the class name on a 'splash' shaped card and attach to the top of the list. Display the list low enough for the children to read and point to it comfortably.

Names Box

Cover a shoe box, or a similar item, with coloured paper. Write each child's name on a coloured sticky label to decorate the box. Then pass the box round at carpet time to see if the children can recognise their name or the name of a friend as the names become more familiar.

Use the box like a giant die to select children for class jobs. Roll it and, with eyes closed, point to a name on the top face.

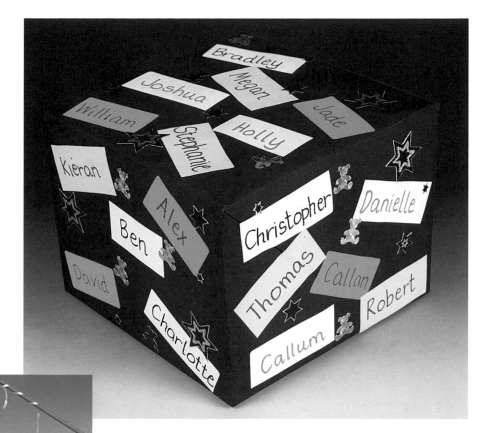

Big Fish in the Pond!

Play fishing for names. Cut out fish shapes from paper and draw a mouth and eyes. Either help the children to write their names on the fish or write the names yourself. Then write your own name on a bigger fish. Slip a paper-clip onto each one. Cut a long piece of card approximately 15 centimetres deep for the pond. Ask older children to decorate both sides with pictures of fish and pond weed before stapling the ends together to make a circle. Make a fishing rod from a piece of stiff art paper rolled diagonally into a tight stick shape, secured with adhesive tape. Tie a magnet to the rod with a length of wool about 20 centimetres long. Can each child 'catch' his or her own name?

Tracing Books

Write the children's names in black pen on white cards measuring about 20 centimetres by 10 centimetres. Staple about 20 sheets of tracing paper to the inside of a folded piece of wrapping paper or a greetings card to make a book. Make sure the book is large enough for a name card to fit easily between the sheets. Write the child's name on a label on the front of the book. Supply felt-tipped pens, which produce a clear line, for the children to trace their names and some simple patterns and shapes.

Rhymes and Poems

If we can instil a passionate interest in stories and rhymes in young children, we are giving them a lifelong interest and a valuable learning tool. We can also spark off a fascination and inquisitiveness about the very bones of these creations – the words – and so be on the way to developing good spellers, too.

We know that poetry has a rhythm, and that it often rhymes, but there can also be rhythm in the way a story is written, especially in those with repeated phrases such as the Giant's, 'Fee Fi Fo Fum!' in *Jack and the Beanstalk*. Children need to be drenched in rhyme and rhythm to encourage an awareness of the patterning of words. If we also actively show them that by changing phonemes we change the word and its use, we are beginning an education in phonics to fuel creative language work.

Start off by developing listening skills and concentration, and a fascination with whole words through activities that use rhyme and rhythm. See page 71 for lists of stories and rhymes that will be particularly useful.

Rhyme Room

Set up a 'Rhyme room' or listening corner. Use the corner of a room, or angle two cupboards to create a corner. Alternatively, fix a tall sheet of corrugated card around a table so that it extends upwards and around to create a screen. Display appropriate texts and the children's own work, and a selection of books. Provide a tape recorder with connections for two or more headsets and a collection of taped traditional stories, rhymes and poems, or the children's own poems. Allow pairs of children to use the corner, so that listening is an enjoyable shared activity.

Rhyming Pairs Game

Cut out an even number (about 20) of large white flash cards. Use pictures from magazines, or older children's drawings, to illustrate each card with one of a pair of items that rhyme, for example draw a mane on one card and a plane on another. Another pair could represent hair and a bear (for the purposes of this exercise it is rhyme and not rime that is important, as the children are listening for sounds). Write the word on the front of the card and later show the children that although the phonemes are the same, the graphemes are not.

Use the cards to play a simple matching game such as 'Snap'. Alternatively, show a matching pair with two decoys for the children to choose the correct pair by saying the words. These games can be played with a class, a group or by individuals.

Pairs of Pictures

Have a brainstorming session with the children to think of pairs of rhyming words that can be illustrated. Fold a sheet of paper in half to make a book shape and ask the children to draw a picture in each half. Write the word underneath each picture and attach all the pairs with adhesive tape to create a zigzag book.

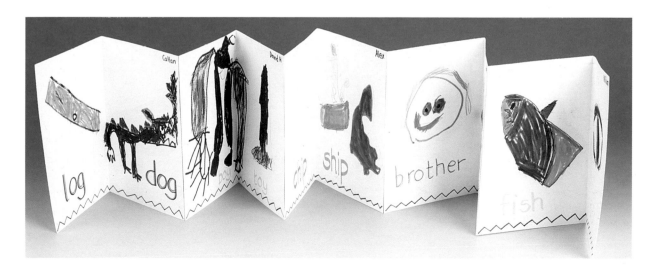

Rhyme Boxes

Children like to open boxes, lift flaps and explore. Use this curiosity to highlight rhyme by putting poems in a box.

Use a lidded shallow box and cover any adverts with paper as shown. Use adhesive tape to attach the lid to the box on its longest side so that it opens like a door. Write the title on the front of the 'door', and some rhyming words or a familiar poem behind the 'door'. Inside the box, glue an older child's illustration or a picture cut out of an old rhyme book. Alternatively, write just the rhyming words in large print. Staple the box onto a backing.

Using knowledge of the text, children can read the titles, open the 'door' and read the poem or the rhyming words.

Rhyme Garden

This garden display is a useful method for recording favourite rhymes, types of poetry or rhyming words. When you say a poem, point to the relevant words on the petals.

For each flower, cut five large petals from coloured card, a circle for the centre and some leaves. Draw a small picture on the centre of the flower to give a clue to the rhyme, or write its title there. Write or glue the rhyming words on the petals. Make a stem by tightly rolling a sheet of green paper. Fix this to the back of the flower and attach the leaves with adhesive tape. Fill a green plastic window box with sand. Stand the flowers up in the sand and cover the sand with crumpled brown tissue paper.

River of Rhymes

Record favourite poems and rhymes on this river.

Draw parallel wavy lines in black pen on a large piece of pale blue paper and cut the paper to a matching wavy shape. Help the children to write the titles of their favourite rhymes along the waves. Display it in the rhyme room or listening corner.

Use the same style of display for whole rhymes or write the rhyming words from a well-known rhyme on each line.

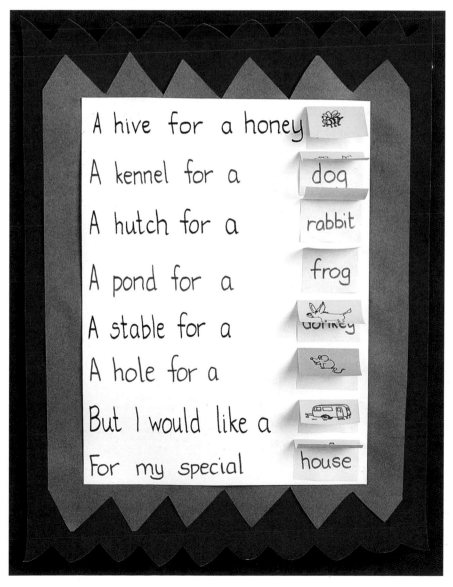

Peepings

Use a large piece of white or pale coloured paper and write out a well-known rhyme or poem on it, leaving a 10 centimetre space before and after each rhyming word. Use a poem with rhyming words that are easy to illustrate, such as 'Hey diddle, diddle' for which you can illustrate 'moon' and 'spoon', for example. Note that the rhyming words are not always at the end of a line. Fix a flap of paper with adhesive tape so that it is hinged above the word. On the front of this you can draw a simple picture to illustrate the word.

Read the poem out with the class. After reading it out a few times, help individuals to read out a line each. Alternatively, lift up the flaps and ask individuals to read the final words.

Poetic Borders

Ask the children to draw their favourite rhyme characters in black pen. Make some photocopies of each illustration and mount them around a display board in a repeat pattern. The display can then be used for some of the following activities:

- Mount a different poem in the centre of the display each week. Read this together with the children and then ask individuals to attempt a performance.
- Make a list of four or five rhyming words with the children and mount on the display. Have a mime quiz and ask the children to read the word you are miming. Make it fun with a group of words like 'tum, hum, mum, sum'.
- Look at the illustrations and identify the poems represented. Why did the artists choose these images?
- Identify the rhyming words in each of the illustrated poems and write these words on paper to display in the centre. Restrict this to just one poem per session.

Shaped Books

Shaped books linked to a theme are interesting for children to use. Staple together three or four sheets of plain paper to form a portrait or landscape book, depending on the shape you are going to draw. To make the top sheet into a front cover, draw the shape yourself, ask older children to draw and colour it or help your pupils to draw individual shapes to make their own books. Fill out the paper with the shape and cut out the excess, cutting through all the pages at once.

For class use, write poems or rhyming words inside the book and decorate the page edges with illustrations. For individuals, photocopy a poem for them to cut out, stick in the book and illustrate.

Carousel

Poems and rhymes, children's pictures of characters, rhyming families or pictures of rhyming words can all be presented on this carousel device.

Use three large sheets of thick, coloured paper. Fold each sheet in half and staple two sheets along the fold, back to back to make an open book. Fix the third sheet to these by gluing along the spine. Cut out pictures from old greetings cards and type up the text using the school style.

Introducing the Alphabet

The idea that shapes represent sounds and speech is central to the concept of reading and writing. We can link what we see (read), hear, say and write by adopting an interdisciplinary approach and using some of the following activities. It seems most effective to identify both the upper- and lower-case forms of letters since the children will see upper-case forms as soon as they become familiar with their names. School policy will be your guide as to whether you teach the sounds and the names of the letters together.

Sounds Corner

Dedicate a corner of the room to sounds. Provide alphabet books and display an alphabet frieze along with some of the displays described on the following pages. Create your own or use a commercial alphabet frieze. If any of the letters on a purchased frieze do not comply with your school style, draw out a letter and stick it over the top. Display the frieze near to your carpet area so that you can refer to it in language sessions.

Peter Pointer

Cut a frame or hand-shaped pointer out of card and decorate. Using reusable adhesive, stick it beside your 'letter of the day' on an alphabet frieze. Move the pointer each day when a new letter is the focus.

Washing Line

Cut out 26 simple clothes shapes from coloured paper. Choose a suitable size for the shapes according to the size of the room and the height at which they are to be hung. Using a black pen, write upper- and lower-case letter pairs (for example, Aa) on each shape. Tightly roll sheets of coloured paper and staple them across a room corner as 'washing lines'. Use clothes pegs to attach the clothes to the lines in rows.

Ask the children to spot the letters you are focusing on by using a pointer. Alternatively, take a 'focus' letter off the line and fix it temporarily to the board for practising letters and words. High-frequency words, starting with each letter, can be added to the bottom of each clothes shape.

Variation

Make bunting, as above, but hang the flag shapes onto lengths of thick, coloured wool. Hang against a wall (see photograph below).

Flags

Cut white paper into 20- by 10-centimetre rectangles. Fold these in half to produce 10-centimetre squares. Write upper- and lower-case letter pairs on one side and draw a simple illustration of an object which begins with that sound on the other. Fix each flag to a long plastic straw using adhesive tape. Decorate empty tins with bright sticky-backed plastic (one for each table in the room) and stand five or six flags in each tin. Swap the flags every few days.

Play 'I Spy the Flag'. Point to a letter on the alphabet line or frieze and ask the children to find and hold up the matching flag.

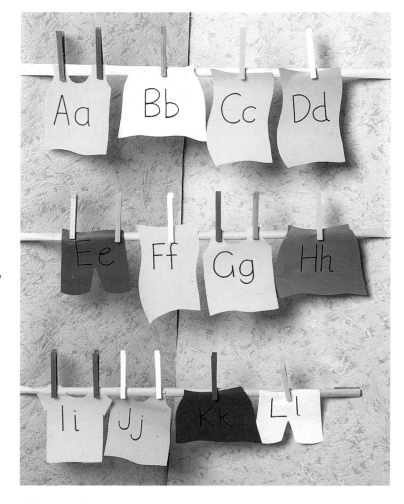

Alphabet Alcove

Paint a strong, medium-sized cardboard box inside and out, or cover in one colour of paper. Stand the box on its side. Fold a piece of card to make a triangular bracket and stand it on the top of the box. Draw round an upper- and lower-case letter template on white card, cut them out, then spread one side of each with glue and cover in glitter. Mount the lower-case letter centrally on one face of the triangular bracket and mount the upper-case letter to the bottom of the box. Now use the box to display three or four items, the names of which start with the chosen letter. Label the items.

Alphabet Mittens

Use glitter glue pens to write an upper- and lower-case letter pair on an old mitten. Alternatively, cut out letters from card and stick one to each mitten with strong glue. Write the upper-case letter on one side of the mitten and the lower-case letter on the other side. Make sure the letters are large and bold. Repeat with different letters on as many mittens as you have available (you do not need to include the whole alphabet, perhaps just the vowels, consonants, or any confusing letters).

If you have all the alphabet, play a matching game with the alphabet frieze. Give a mitten to each child, then point to a letter and ask who has the matching letter. Alternatively, play 'Auntie Alphabet asks'. Ask: 'Who has the sound I am pointing to?' 'I'm pointing to "a". Who has me on their hand?'

The Letters

Most children learn to read and write some words before they begin to learn any phonic rules. This sight vocabulary can be enlarged steadily and used alongside any teaching of the phonic rules. We can start this programme by introducing the letters of the alphabet using a multi-disciplinary approach. The following ideas can be used for activities involving hearing the sounds and reading and writing the letters.

Alphabet Rainbow

Create a fabric wall-hanging that displays the alphabet, with the vowels and consonants decorated to differentiate them. Use the display to identify letters and to teach alphabetical order.

If possible, to allow for practice, use fabric paint that is painted onto paper first and then ironed onto the fabric when dry, rather than paint that is put directly onto the fabric. Best results will be obtained from using polycotton – dye may fade from other fabrics. Completely cover five sheets of paper with assorted colours before painting two sheets with a single plain colour. Allow them all to dry thoroughly.

Use large letter stencils to draw the alphabet letters on the unpainted sides of the paper (so that the letters will be the right way round when ironed). Use the consonant stencils on the patterned paper and the vowel stencils on the plain paper. Cut out the letters.

Cut a piece of polyester-cotton large enough to accommodate the whole alphabet, allowing for a 15 centimetre border at the top and bottom. Turn these borders over and sew to make a hem of about 7 centimetres. Iron the letters onto the cotton in alphabetical order.

Thread lengths of doweling through the top and bottom hems and tie on thick, strong wool for hanging.

⚠ **Note:** Children should be well-supervised or kept away from hot irons when used.

3D Letter Display

Focus attention on the 'letters of the week' by making these 3D items which can then be displayed near your discussion area. Allow the children to handle them carefully while you identify the letter on each, and brainstorm words starting with that sound. Use the 3D items to focus on any problem letters, too.

Cover or paint a small tin or box with a plain colour and then cut out and stick on a lower-case letter in a contrasting colour. Ask older children to draw and cut out illustrations of items which have the same initial letter as the one chosen, and to cover the tin or box with them. Label the pictures, highlighting the initial letter. Use one side of the tin or box to list words that start with the letter.

Bouncing Letters

This is a small and easy-to-make device that attracts attention and is highly memorable.

Draw the letters you are studying on stiff, shiny card and cut them out. Next, cut strips of clear, curved plastic from a soft drinks bottle. Fix the letters onto one end of the strips with adhesive tape. Staple the other ends of the strips to a display board in a position where the letters can be bounced and talked about.

Make the upper- and lower-case forms of one letter at a time and display them beside a list of high-frequency words starting with that letter, or a picture of a familiar character whose name begins with the letter. Display in the Handwriting House (see page 66) near writing practice sheets.

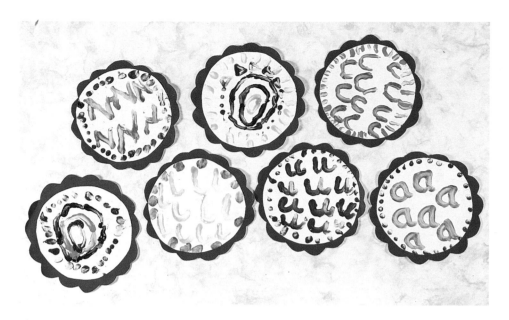

Finger-painted Letters

Mix PVA glue with ready-mixed paint or use one of the pearlised paints available. Using a glossy paper, if possible, cut out circles approximately 20 centimetres in diameter. Put the paints in flat palettes and provide a cloth for wiping fingers between colours. Tell the children to pick a favourite letter, or a new letter, and use an index finger to write the letter shapes on the paper.

Decorate the edges and display them as 'letter flowers'. Children will be able to talk about these and so gain extra exposure to letters.

You may wish to encourage the children to choose letters that are formed in a particular way. For example: rounded letters, ascenders and descenders.

Printing Letters

Expanded polystyrene 3D letters (available as bath toys) can be used as printing blocks if you add a 'handle'. Use hot glue to attach a small piece of wood or wide cotton reel to the back of the letter. Use the printing blocks to allow the children to print their own names, or rows of letters, on strips of coloured paper to make a display.

Variation

Cut out simple shapes from coloured paper. Each shape should be the outline of an item that begins with a chosen letter. Using the printing blocks above, print the relevant letters on the outlines. Encourage the children to use one letter and one colour only on each shape.

Fishing Game

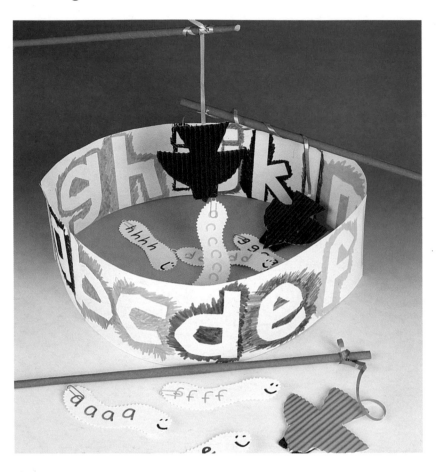

To make a 'pond', cut a strip of thin card to about 15 centimetres by 1 metre and help the children to decorate it. Use masking tape to form the lower-case letters and then colour all over the edges of the letters with felt-tipped pens. Remove the tape to reveal white letters. Staple the ends of the strip together to make a circle.

Make fishing rods by rolling large pieces of coloured paper into tight rolls and securing with adhesive tape. Tie 40-centimetre lengths of thick wool or tape to horseshoe magnets, then cut out bird-shaped pieces of card and stick them onto the magnets. Tie and glue the other ends of the wool to the 'rods'. To make 'water worms', select four letters from those you are learning and write each one several times on six small worm-shapes cut from card. Attach a paper-clip to each worm.

To play the game, two children take turns to fish out all of two kinds of letters, for example all the 'o' and 'a' worms.

Highlighting Labels

When labelling a collection of words on a picture, highlight the initial letter in a contrasting colour and use the picture in discussions. On the picture shown, the initial letter colour has been matched with the colour to be labelled.

To establish the idea of a phonics system and to give the children some rules to work with when spelling their own words it helps to start by teaching the initial sounds of words. Show the written letter, say the commonest sound this letter makes (like 'c' as in 'cat' and not 'circle') and present a concrete word with that initial letter. At the earliest stages it can also help to use a picture so that the child has a visual clue for the word. Although many children can write some words before they know all the initial sounds, and can certainly read words in excess of this, it is preferable that they know most sounds before progressing to word building.

Sounds Shop

This shop can be used for role-play and to help with the teaching of the initial sounds of words. Encourage the children to help you make it, to give them maximum exposure to the sounds, letters and words.

Cover five shoe boxes with paper or paint. Use PVA glue to fix them together in a staggered arrangement to represent shelves. Secure to the top of a small table with brown parcel tape or clear, wide adhesive tape. Select five letters that you are currently learning and find three or four toys or other items that start with each letter. Display as shown. Add a label with the items listed and the initial sound of each highlighted in a different colour. Provide a toy cash till with 'coins' made from card with the appropriate letters on them.

Encourage the children to role-play the shop owner who sells the items displayed, and the shoppers who have to pay by using the correct 'coin' for a particular item, for example a 't' coin for a teddy bear. Change the collection regularly to keep it fresh and to co-ordinate with other phonic work.

Sorting Letters

To make a letter tray, spray an egg box with gold paint, adding glitter for extra decoration. Cut out 30 leaf-shaped colour cards about 4 centimetres in length. Choose six letters and write each letter on six cards with a black pen.

Ask the children to sort the letters by putting the same letters into one hole of the letter tray. Encourage them to look at the letter shapes.

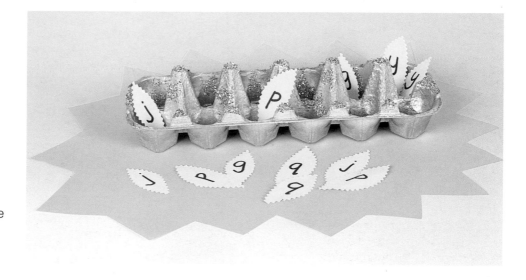

Confusing Pairs

There are some pairs of letters that can confuse children because of a similarity of sound or shape and method of formation. For example, the letters 'j' and 'g' can make exactly the same sound if the 'g' is soft, and both also have a descending tail. The pairs of letters that are most often confused are: b/d, g/j, m/n, h/n, c/k, c/s, u/v, a/d, b/p, p/q (lower case) and H/I, J/T, M/N, O/Q, V/W (upper case).

To help reduce the chances of confusion, pronounce sounds very clearly and slowly; encourage the children to copy the letters clearly, with well-defined ascenders and descenders; and encourage the children to say the sound as they write and use each letter. Once the alphabet has been introduced and the children are fairly confident with letter formation, try the following activities to prevent or reduce confusion.

Puzzling Pairs

This is an interactive visual aid to help children discriminate between potentially confusing pairs. Its novelty may help the children to memorise the correct usage. For easy daily reference, display several on a large piece of card, folded to make a triptych.

You will need sheets of card and sheets of white paper. Cut two flaps in each card and write a pair of letters that are often confused on the front of the flaps. On the underside of each flap, write a simple word which has the chosen initial letter. (The words should be nouns that are easy to illustrate and easy for children to read.) Trim the paper sheets to a slightly smaller size and glue them to the back of each card. Where the paper shows under the flaps, ask older children to draw an illustration to represent each word.

Tracing Pairs

Make tracing books so that the children can trace one of any pair of letters with which they become confused. Make the tracing books as described on page 7. Then cut ten pieces of card the same size as the tracing book. On each one, write a row of one letter, a reference word and a picture. Draw a baseline on the cards in a different colour to introduce the idea of ascenders and descenders.

Clinging Pairs

Letters that can represent two sounds, such as vowels in their long and short forms, can be confusing. Other examples of letters that represent more than one sound include 'y' ('daddy', 'sky', 'yellow', 'yummy'); 'c' ('cat', 'cinema', 'circle'); and 'g' ('go', 'giant').

This display can be used as a visual aid whenever you want to talk about or use these 'confusing pairs' as graphemes or phonemes to illustrate the pair in question. For example, if a child confuses the capital 'G' in a friend's name 'Gordon' with the sound and appearance of the lower-case 'c', clip animals to the side of the letters in question.

Take a piece of stiff white card, 1 metre by 10 centimetres. Leaving a clear space of about 20 centimetres either side and 10 centimetres at the top and bottom of the card, draw a ladder with a thick, coloured felt-tipped pen. The ladder must have 26 spaces between its rungs. Write the lower case letters in black pen. Make a second ladder for the capitals in the same way. You will then need two clinging animals for each ladder – perhaps tiny toys with arm clips or magnetic legs.

23

Introducing the Vowels

Introduce the vowels – a, e, i, o and u – as a family of letters, each of which represents two sounds: a short and a long sound. Use some of the following ideas to introduce them as the initial letters in words (although there are very few single-letter long-vowels at the beginning of words appropriate for young children).

Vowel Umbrella

You need a brightly coloured child's umbrella for this display, which can be hung from the ceiling or propped in a pot of gravel or sand.

Cut out large vowels from brightly coloured paper. Attach the letters to the umbrella with double-sided adhesive tape, using one umbrella panel for each letter and leaving sections between the letters empty, if necessary. Cut out five raindrop shapes from white card. Use one raindrop for each vowel and on one side write about three words that start with the long vowel sound and on the reverse, using a different coloured pen, write three words that start with the short sound. Names could be included. Hang the raindrops from the bottom of each matching letter panel using thin strips of paper and adhesive tape or coloured wool. Add more words as they come up in reading or writing.

Children's Names

Draw a large black outline of an animal and photocopy it four times. Within each outline, list names beginning with the main vowels. If possible, use children's names from within your class or school and include names that use the short and long sounds, such as Aiden and Anne, Evie and Edward. Display in alphabetical order in a row for reference and discussion.

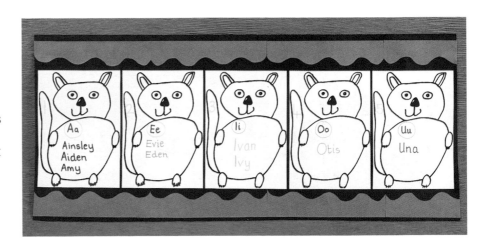

Sliding Window

Write the vowels in a row on a piece of stiff card. Make a sliding frame from a square of contrasting coloured card. Cut three sides of a square in the middle of the card and bend back the square along the fourth side, creating a flap to hang the frame over the row of vowels.

This can be used to focus attention on a particular vowel.

The Vowel Bunch

Make five paper-plate puppet heads by gluing on collage materials for facial features, hair and jewellery. Cut out a bow tie from coloured card for each and attach a vowel sound. On the reverse of each 'head' write the full name of the puppet. Pick two names that start with the long vowel, such as Amy Apron, Eva Evening, Ivan Icicle, Otis Ocean and Una Uniform.

Use these as visual aids in activities:

- Help the children make up stories about the characters, using words with the same initial vowel sound. For example: Ivan Icicle comes from an infant school in Iceland but is going on holiday to India where he is looking for an important ice cream factory.
- Let the puppets conduct well-known tunes as the children sing vowel sounds in place of the words.
- Sing 'Old Macdonald' with a puppet's sound in place of the animal sound, for example: 'With an e e here, an e e there, here an e, there an e ...'

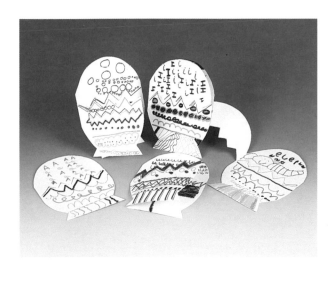

'Eggciting' Vowels

This display helps to introduce the two types of vowel sounds (long and short) and should be done after some discussion and a brainstorming session to discover words that start with each sound.

Fold a rectangular sheet of card in half, widthways. Draw and cut round an egg-in-a-cup shape, leaving the fold side intact to make a hinge. Cut the front section into two halves, following a zigzag line, remembering to position the cut so that the sections above and below the cut are hinged separately. Decorate the lower half as an egg-cup. Decorate the upper half with one of the vowels in both lower and upper case. Let each child pick one vowel for their egg.

Fold back the top and bottom sections. Inside, draw a picture of an object that starts with the short vowel sound and one that starts with the long sound. Add the words, too, using a different colour to highlight the initial letter.

Racing Sounds

Collect five small wind-up plastic toys that move in a fairly straight line. Stick a self-adhesive label on each and write one of the vowels on each with a different coloured pen. Give each one a name that starts with the long vowel sound and sounds the letter alone, such as Amy A, Easy E, Icy I, Old O and Uniform U.

Hold desk-top races and cheer on the competitors.

Alliteration

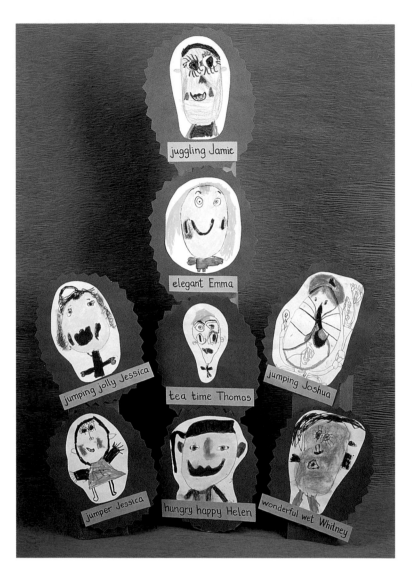

Alliteration is a language concept which can help develop children's phonological awareness and their knowledge of the alphabet. It is simply a phrase or sentence in which adjacent or closely connected words begin with the same sound.

If the children are tuned into the idea of changing sounds being entertaining through working with rhymes and songs, they will quickly understand how alliteration works. You can provide many amusing examples to whet their appetite, the main value at this stage being in speaking and listening.

Our Names

Find pictures of cartoon and story book characters that have alliterative names, such as Donald Duck, Daffy Duck, Mickey Mouse, Postman Pat and Sooty and Sweep. Emphasise the initial sounds and write some of the names on the board with the initial letters in a contrasting colour. Give a few alliterative examples using the children's own names, by adding a positive adjective, such as Sunny Sue, Terrific Tina, Peter Perfect, Radiant Rani and Ticklish Tom.

Ask the children to paint self-portraits and label them with the alliterative names. Incorporate them into a display to illustrate sounds of the alphabet.

City Street

Make a frieze of the children's drawings or paintings of shops laid out horizontally like a city street. Write alliterative shop signs above each shop, such as Tim's Trainers and Bill's Bikes. Use the frieze as a background for role-play.

Delicious Dinners

Look at a school dinner or restaurant menu and rewrite it using alliterative names. For example, 'sausages' could become 'sizzling sausages'; other examples could include jumping jelly, chilly chips, bouncing beans and power pizza. Decorate it with paintings of the items and add a border of printed letters (see page 19).

Listen to Tongue Twisters

Teach the children to say some well-known tongue twisters, such as 'Peter Piper', 'Betty Botter bought some butter' and 'She sells sea shells'. Can the children discriminate between the 's' and 'sh' sounds? Tell the children that you are listening for sounds at the beginning of words that are the same. See if they can identify the alliterative words when listening. Next, write out a single line of one rhyme, highlighting the initial sound. Point to this as you say the poem together. Both 'Peter Piper' and 'Betty Botter' have alliterative sounds in the middle of the words, too, and these may confuse. Say these words slowly and train the ear with two or three words at a time, for example 'picked a peck', emphasising the 'p'. Make up one or two more tongue twister poems or sentences and record them on tape for the 'Listening Corner', for example:

'Sister Suzy sizzles in the sunshine,
Sizzling and fizzling all day long.
If Suzy sizzled sausages in the sun
She'd have enough to fill her tum.'

Walk Along a Tongue Twister

Write out a complete tongue twister poem, such as 'Peter Piper', on long strips of pastel-coloured paper, using black, and a contrasting colour for all the initial letter 'p'. Display it in a long line on the floor so that the children can walk beside it from left to right, following the poem and identifying the alliterative letters as they read.

Variation

Create new tongue twisters as a group game. Begin with a name such as 'Silly Sally' and add an alliterative verb ('sizzles') or use two names and one verb, ('Sally sees Sue'). Offer the children alternative verbs, plus decoys (such as 'skids', 'eats', 'sings', 'slips', 'skips', 'runs'). They select the one that alliterates and sounds the funniest. Continue in this way until a number of alliterative phrases have been made. Use them to make up a collection of 'silly sentences'.

Alphabetical Order

Now that you have introduced the alphabet and started to teach the children how to identify and use letters, knowledge of their definitive order will help them to progress further – they will be able to use word books, wall dictionaries and lists. The following devices can be used to help develop the concept of alphabetical order.

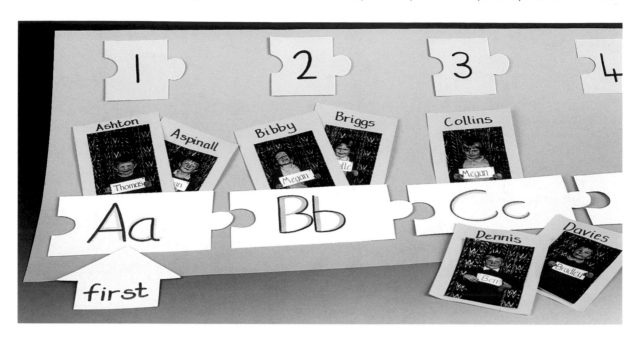

Children's Alphabet

Using photographs of the children and their own names helps to give meaning to this alphabet presentation.

Cut out 26 jigsaw-shaped coloured cards and write an upper- and lower-case pair of letters of the alphabet on each as shown. Staple these in alphabetical order onto a display board to create pockets. Position them low enough for the children to reach. Glue a photograph of each child onto a piece of card and make sure both their fore and surnames appear on the card. Sort the pictures into the pockets according to their surname. Reinforce the numerical order by adding numbers and arrow-shaped labels, 'first' and 'last'.

Alphabet Train

Ask older children to draw a train engine and a carriage using a black felt-tipped pen. Photocopy 25 carriages and write a letter of the alphabet in both upper- and lower-case on each carriage in different colours. Number each carriage, too, and display them in order behind the engine. Add a directional arrow under the engine and a card pocket to each carriage. Next, cut out card figures and label each with an upper- and lower-case letter. Add facial features. Match the letters on the figures with those on the carriages, so the people can 'take a ride'.

Use this device as an alphabet frieze for reading, for looking at alphabetical order and for playing spotting games by asking who can say the letter sound after 'd' or the letter sound before 'y', and so on. Alternatively, ask the children to match the card figures with those on the train. Swap the cards round and repeat. To make a dictionary, on each figure write a list of high-frequency words and other words that come up in writing.

Printed Alphabet Borders

Use printing blocks (see page 19) and paints to print the letters in alphabetical order on strips of coloured paper. When dry, draw patterns on the letters with felt-tipped pens for further decoration. Use the strips to frame the children's writing, names, alphabet pictures, self-portraits, and so on.

Variations

Print complete alphabet sets in three single colours. Point to a letter and ask the children to spot it on one of the other coloured alphabet lines. Provide positional clues such as, 'The e sound is at the beginning of the alphabet on the (red) strip. Look at the beginning of your (blue) strip. Can you find an e?' Encourage numerical ordering by adding a number line above a set of letters and asking the children to 'find the letter number 1' or to 'say the letter that is number 20', and so on. The printed letters can also be used above lists of children's names and familiar words. The lists can be displayed together as a class dictionary.

Sliders

Use this device to highlight one letter at a time on a linear display of the alphabet. Let the children move it when you ask them to find a letter, for example, 'the letter after m'.

Cut five strips of strong white card 60 by 8 centimetres. Write or print the letters on them as shown.

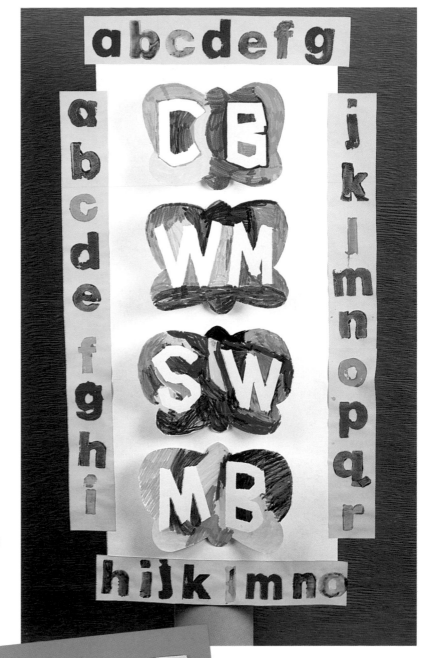

Leave space around the edges for stapling and space between the letters. Cut out a body shape with its arms hanging down, sized approximately 12 by 9 centimetres as shown. Staple or glue the ends of the letter strips to a backing and sit the slider on top of a letter.

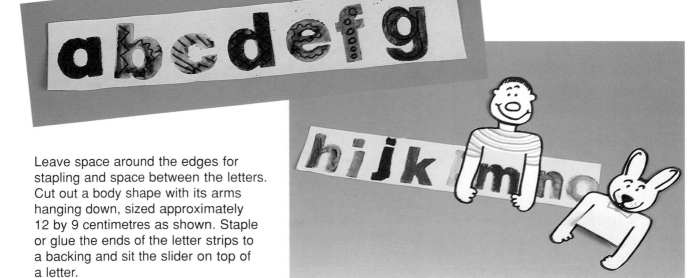

29

My Initials

Ask the children to find the initial letters for their first and last names on an alphabet line and to discuss where the two are in relation to each other. Does anyone have both names starting with the same initial?

Make displays of the children's initials. Fold a sheet of card in half and cut out a symmetrical shape, such as a butterfly. Help the children to form a capital on each side by tearing off strips of masking tape 2 centimetres in width and sticking them onto the card. Use assorted felt-tipped pens to completely cover the tape and white card with colours. Make sure no spaces are left and the colour is right up to the edges of the tape. Strip off the tape to reveal the initials in white. Display them alongside the alphabet.

Dot-to-dot

To help establish the concept of alphabetical order, create your own black and white copies of dot-to-dot pictures, using lower-case letters in alphabetical order, instead of numbers. To create a dot-to-dot picture, draw a simple picture in pencil, adding some details and the dots and letters evenly spaced and in their correct order. Draw over the dots, letters and some of the picture details in ink, then erase the pencil lines before photocopying. Supply the children with sharp pencils or fine felt-tipped pens for joining the dots in the correct order.

Make a booklet of five to ten pictures for each child. Include some alphabet pictures that show only five letters in sequence, such as d e f g h.

Three-letter Words

Once the children are confident enough to identify and write most of the letters of the alphabet, it is time to introduce the notion that they can spell words on their own (some will already have tried). Begin with phonically regular, three-letter words which have a consonant-vowel-consonant (c-v-c) structure. The following ideas offer opportunities to focus on the spelling of these simple words.

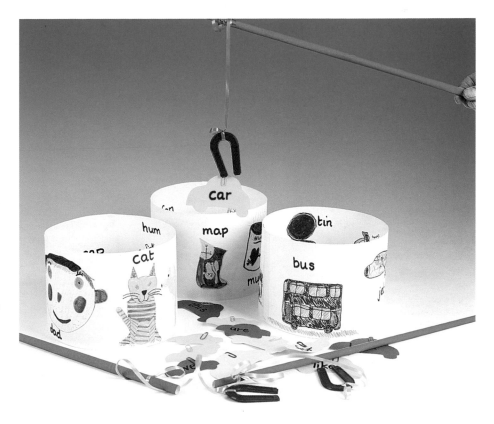

Word Crane

This is a game to help identify initial, final or medial letters.

Ask older children to decorate a long rectangular sheet of white paper on both sides with illustrations depicting the c-v-c words you have chosen. Join the narrow ends of the rectangle with two paper-clips to create a 'pit'. To make 'scrap cars', cut out simple car-shapes from 6 by 4 centimetre cards and write a word on each. Fix a paper-clip to each car so that it can be lifted. Make two 'crane jibs' from tightly rolled and glued sheets of paper and then tie and glue a length of tape to the stick. Tie a horseshoe magnet to the free end of the tape.

To play the game, let the children use a crane to pick up words with specified initial, final or medial letters. The game can be played in pairs or as a group.

Word Link

This is a linear jigsaw that identifies the initial and final sounds of words and helps children to focus on them.

For a five-word game, cut five jigsaw shapes out of strong white card. On each, write words that can be linked by common final and initial letters, for example cat–tap–pen–nod–dog. Ask older children to illustrate each word or glue on a picture cut from greetings cards. For each set that you make, put the same numeral on the back so that sets can be kept intact. Store in plastic wallets. Read the words using the picture cues, emphasising the initial and final sounds and looking for the links.

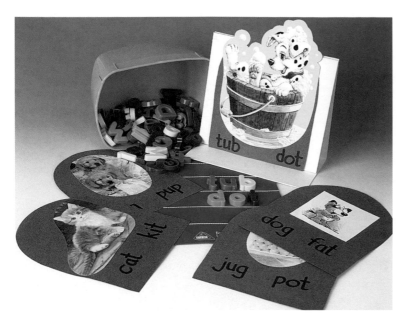

Magnawords

You will need a magnetic board and magnetic lower-case letters. Cut out pictures from old greetings cards to illustrate c-v-c words. Glue them onto coloured paper and label with two appropriate words. Make a stand to rest them on by folding strong card into a prism shape.

Ask the children to work in pairs and make the sets of two words using magnetic letters. Each child can check the other is right. Ask them to read the words, by using the picture clues and sounding out individual letters.

Word Building

Make a triangular word holder by placing a rectangle of thin card horizontally on a table and folding the top and bottom edges in towards the centre. Gather the folded edges together and squash the shape gently to form a pyramid base. Attach the folded edges together at the ends, leaving a slit along the top to hold cards. Make picture cards of concrete objects depicting simple c-v-c words. Make consonant letter cards from white card approximately 8 by 4 centimetres. Use coloured card for the vowels. Tell the children to make three-letter words using one coloured letter card as the middle letter.

Little Boxes

These boxes can be used for word sorting and to help children focus on letter position. Cover five small matchboxes with different coloured paper. Decide which letter position to target, then write a letter on each box. Make the appropriate letter cards to fit the boxes, writing the words in the same colour as covers the relevant matchbox. For example, tell the children that all the boxes show the middle letter of words, so the word cards they collect for the 'a' box might include 'bat', 'man', 'dad' and 'tan'. Similarly, the letter on the box could be said to be the final letter of the words to be collected.

Huge Letters

Cut out a huge letter from coloured paper. Then ask the children to draw pictures of things starting with that letter and to write the word. Mount the pictures on the huge letter for display.

Variation

Cut out large letters from coloured card and write c-v-c words that begin with those letters on the appropriate cut out.

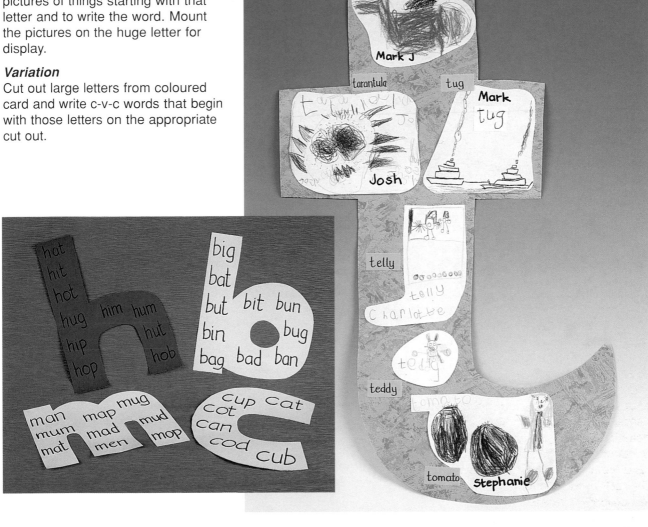

Word Concertinas

Fold long strips of white paper five times into concertinas. Work with a small group to brainstorm c-v-c words starting with specific letters. Make a list of five or six words with a separate letter for each child. Give each child a list to copy and illustrate, with one word on each fold of the concertina. Attach the concertinas to a board for display.

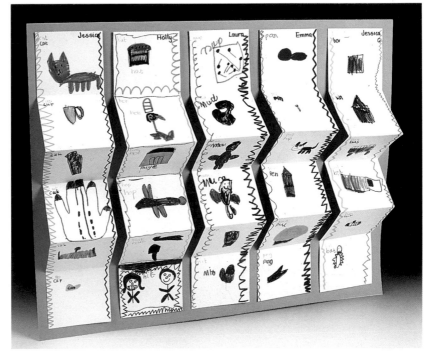

33

Onset and Rime

The following activities and devices introduce the concept of 'onset and rime'. At this level, the 'onset' can be explained as the first single sound of the word. This might be a single letter, a blend like 'bl' or a digraph such as 'ch'. The 'rime' is that part of a syllable or word that has the vowel and the final consonant or consonant cluster. So, in the word 'cat', 'c' is the onset and 'at' the·rime. The sounds of rhyme will help the children to discriminate between the onset and rime. Rhyming words can be displayed in a number of imaginative ways, as in the 'Rhyming Rocket' above (see page 36 for a description on how to make this).

Words and Bricks

Use contact glue and strong card to set up the activity as shown. Sit a rime brick on a board and show the children how to change the word by changing the 'onset'. Decide which c-v-c rime or rimes you want to use, perhaps starting with 'a' words and words that end, for example, with 'ab' and 'ad'. Focus on just two or three rimes at first. Emphasise that the ending stays the same and the words all rhyme. Once the children can do this and read the words, give them small pieces of paper to write one or two words on. Change the cards to new onsets and rimes when necessary.

Words and Pictures Concertina

Make this display to use as a reminder of the possible rhyming quality of c-v-c words.

Fold a sheet of paper in half to make a booklet. Brainstorm rhyming c-v-c words that can be illustrated. Draw the picture for each word in the pair and write the words underneath. Older children can help with the illustrations.

Display several in a horizontal concertina format. Periodically, produce new concertina booklets with new words and pictures to demonstrate the rhyming quality of rimes.

Word Sliders

To make these, use a piece of card approximately 16 by 18 centimetres. Cut two slits into the card, leaving space between to write the onsets in a vertical line. Glue the outside edges of the back of the base onto another piece of strong card. Then cut a 15 by 3 centimetre strip from contrasting coloured card. Write the rime on the strip before sliding it through the slits in the base.

Make a collection of word sliders to show rimes with all the vowels. Children can write down each rime list they make.

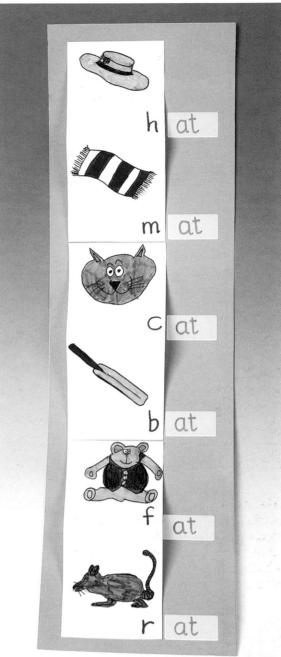

Folders

These folders focus attention on the onset and the rime separately and also ask for whole words to be written.

Design a grid on a sheet of paper and fold as shown. List the onsets and rimes, using the fold to divide them physically. The children can write the complete word in the spaces on the right. You can vary the rime on each sheet.

Word Lists

Word banks of regular words can be useful when teaching or as a reference for children when they are writing. It could be useful to look at one vowel at a time with all the possible onsets and rimes, then you will not have too many words on display at once. One short list for a short period can also be stimulating as the children will look forward to the arrival of new lists. Word lists can be presented in many interesting and accessible ways.

Wizard

Draw a simple outline of a wizard in a wide, striped robe on a large sheet of white art paper and write rhyming c-v-c words in each stripe.

The display can be used in various activities. For example, encourage the memorising of sounds and spellings by pointing to words on the wizard, covering them up and then asking the children to write the words from memory.

Rhyming Rascals

Cut out a strip of coloured art paper about 50 by 15 centimetres. Fold it 8 or 10 times to create a concertina effect. Draw a head, hands, feet or paws as shown on white paper and colour them if you wish. Glue the head and limbs on to the concertina and then write the list of words, one on each fold. Finish off with a paper bow-tie shape in the centre on which you can write the appropriate rime for the list.

Rhyming Rocket

See photograph on page 34. Cut out a rocket shape from coloured art paper. Add different coloured 'jet streams' about 30 centimetres long, on which you can write different sets of c-v-c words with the same rime. Change just the jet streams as necessary.

Starting Blends

Blends are two or more individual consonants that are pronounced as a smoothly joined double-sound in which both can still be distinguished. They are commonly in the initial or final position in words. Blends are important phonic units, and can often form the 'onset' of a word. To learn to use blends children need to have well-developed hearing and speech development and be familiar with the concept of 'onset' and 'rime'.

The consonant blends are classified according to their dominant phoneme, so 'bl', 'cl', 'fl', 'sl' and 'pl' can be called the initial 'l' blends but 'sn', 'sm', 'st' and 'sk' are the initial 's' blends. To introduce the concept of consonant blends, start with just the common initial blends such as 'l', 'r' and 's' and then final blends, such as 's' and 'n'. A good introduction to initial blends is a brainstorming session in which single consonants are added to c-v-c words.

Blend Bears

This device allows the children to add a whole blend as the onset to a variety of rimes.

Draw a bear shape on stiff brown paper and cut it out. Add a hat in a contrasting colour, on which you can write the blend. Write rimes in boxes on a strip of white card, leaving enough space for the onset to be placed in front. Write the onset on a smaller piece of white card and attach it with coloured wool to one of the bear's paws. The children can pick up the card and place it next to a rime to make a word.

Sound Wheel

This device also distinguishes the onset blend from the rime and children find the 'peep-hole' concept very inviting.

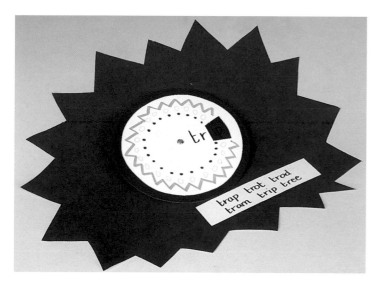

Cut a circle 14 centimetres in diameter from white card and a circle 16 centimetres in diameter from coloured card. Cut a 2 centimetre square peep-hole in the white circle about 1 centimetre from the edge. Loosely secure the white circle onto the coloured circle with a paper-clip so that the card will turn. Write the blend in coloured pen on the top circle and a rime in black pen in the peep-hole. Turn the first rime just out of view and write the second, and so on. For the 'fl' blend you could use these words: fled, flap, flat, flit, flop, flan, flip, flab, flag.

Children turn the wheel to make a new word which they can copy. Make a wheel for each of the initial 'l' blends ('sl', 'pl', 'fl', 'cl', 'bl').

Word Waves

Unusually shaped lists can be memorable. Use a large piece of white paper and draw gentle waves across the bottom using several shades of thick blue felt-tipped pens or crayons and write a blend at the start of each wave. Ask older children to draw and cut out boats. Mount them over the edge of the backing for a 3D effect.

To use the display, start with a brainstorming session to think of words that use one of the blends. Help the children to take turns, writing the words along the correct wave. Fill a different wave at each session, occasionally going back to revise past 'waves'.

Post Boxes

This is a sorting activity. Use small tins with soft lids and cut a 0.5 by 5 centimetre slit in the lid with a craft knife. Decorate the tins with coloured or patterned paper. Write a blend on a coloured label and stick it on the front of the tin. Cut out small 8 by 4 centimetre cards on which to write the words that start with the chosen blend. If you make a container and cards for three different blends, the activity will challenge the children as they 'post' each word into the correct container.

Dingle-dangle Scarecrow

Read 'I'm a Dingle-dangle Scarecrow', a poem which provides an opportunity for reading several initial and final blends.

When all the cows were sleeping, and the sun had gone to bed,
Up jumped the scarecrow and this is what he said:
"I'm a dingle-dangle scarecrow with a flippy, floppy hat
I can shake my hands like this, and stamp my feet like that!"

M and G Russell-Smith

Make a collage of the famous scarecrow with the children, using card, fabric, buttons, felt pieces and straw. Stand the collage in a tin of sand by attaching a cane to the scarecrow's back. Push the cane into the sand and cover the tin with paper. Alternatively, buy a cheap garden ornament and add the decorations shown. Add 'bouncing' parts to the hands and feet on which you can write the blends from the poem. Cut out star-shapes and feet from card and write 'fl', 'sc', 'st', 'sl' – one on each. Cut out four 3 by 10 centimetre plastic strips from a clear plastic drinks bottle. Use adhesive tape to attach a strip to the back of each star and foot shape. Tape these on the scarecrow so that they stand out, allowing the children to bounce them and read them. Add a name label for the scarecrow and a label for his 'flippy, floppy hat'. Write out the poem, or your own version of the poem, using a highlighter pen for the blends.

Read and learn the poem together.

Consonant Digraph sh

The consonant digraphs (sh, ch, th) are new concepts in phonemes for the children as the two letters represent one sound. All three can appear in an initial, medial or final position, for example: sheep, washes, wish.

Shop Display

Introduce the 'sh' phoneme through the medium of a play shop in which everything for sale starts with 'sh'. Make the shop using small covered boxes as shelves and a small table. Label each item, highlighting the 'sh' digraph in a different colour. Add a shop sign using a stick support pushed into a tin of sand or florists' foam. Collect as many 'sh' items to 'sell' as possible, such as shorts, shiny things, sheets of paper, toy sharks and shakers. Use the shop for role-play and shells as currency.

Sheep on the Shore

Make a mini display for the following tongue twisters: 'She sells sea shells on the sea shore' and 'A sunbathing sheep in the shade on the shore'. Place a toy sheep under an umbrella (parasol) on a shore made from several sheets of sandpaper taped together and cut in a curved shape. Add other items as shown.

Follow-up work can include a brainstorming session in which the children try to guess the name of the sheep (following the clue that it begins with 'sh'). They could think of children's names in school, such as Sheena, Sheila, Shelagh, Shelley, Shaun, Shamus and Shane.

Shiny Zigzag Book

Use shiny silver and gold card to make a zigzag book. Make a long list of all the words the children can think of that start with 'sh'. Pick out the nouns for older children to illustrate. Then attach the pictures to the book using reusable adhesive so that the book can be reused as a visual aid in the future.

Sand Writing

Cut out the letters from sand paper and glue them onto strong card. Cut around the letters to form a single unit which represents the single sound of the digraph. Add a dot of paint or glitter glue for starting points and then ask the children to use a finger to trace over the formation of the letters.

Alternatively, ask the children to finger paint the digraph using contact glue. Sprinkle glitter or coloured art sand over the glue to make your own 'sand paper' letters. You could also provide a shallow tray with a little fine sand in the bottom for the children to practise writing 'sh' in.

Handwriting

Make simple handwriting sheets for the children to practise writing 'sh'. Decorate the sheets with pictures of items that start with 'sh'. Provide the opportunity to write the single letters, then the digraph and finally a small selection of words.

Variation
Use the 'sh' word 'sharing' for discussion in personal, social and emotional sessions. Write the word on a single piece of paper, highlighting the 'sh' and display it on a wall near the carpet area.

41

Consonant Digraph ch

The digraph 'ch' can appear at both the beginning and the end of words and can make three sounds, as in 'chip', 'Christmas' and 'Charlotte'. It is useful to introduce the most common sound first, orally, such as 'ch' at the start of words (as in 'chip'). Go on to compile a long list of 'ch' words with the children. Flash cards can be used later to compare 'sh' with 'ch'. Handwriting practice will also emphasise the difference.

Chimps and Chicks Shop

Make a shop that sells just toy chimps and chicks, which the children can bring into school from home. Use the shop as a focus in the following activities:

- Have a brainstorming session to make a list of names for the toys with the common 'ch' (e.g. Chester). Ask the children if any of their families' or friends' names are in this group. Names beginning with the soft 'ch' (e.g. Charlotte) and the hard 'ch' (e.g. Christopher) should be listed separately. Highlight the initial digraph in a contrasting colour.
- Ask the children to draw pictures of their favourite chimp or chick for advertisements in the shop. Encourage them to copy or write a name of their choice under the picture.
- Make up advertising slogans using 'ch' words as shown above.
- Provide toy money and a till and put prices on the toys to link with numeracy work.
- Make a list of 'shop' vocabulary for display nearby (e.g. 'sell', 'buy', 'customer', 'till', 'change', 'money', 'pay', 'checkout').

Zigzags

Make a vertical zigzag list by folding a card concertina and adding a word for each fold. Labels can include adjectives or verbs as well as the noun, for example 'cheeky chicks'. Add simple illustrations or pictures cut out of magazines or old greetings cards. Words that are difficult to illustrate can be written alongside 'family' members, for example 'peach, reach, teach'.

Have a brainstorming session to think of alliterative names (as shown) and phrases. Ask individuals to read out their favourites from the list. The children could also be asked to draw their favourite item and copy or write the appropriate name underneath it.

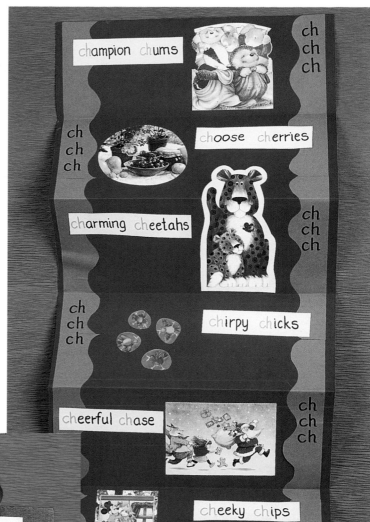

Variation

Create a 'longest list in the world'. Use a long piece of paper about 12 centimetres wide and start off the list with words you have discussed. Then ask the children to bring in from home a single word that starts or ends with 'ch', written on a piece of paper which can be stuck on the list. The children should remember their own word!

Christmas Box

Make a Christmas box poster to illustrate the hard sound of the 'ch' digraph. Write a list of names beginning with the hard 'ch' and display near the box.

Cheerful Charlie Chimp's Café

Make a café that serves only foods that start with the initial 'ch'.

On a small table, stand a large rectangular piece of cardboard folded into a triptych. Small boxes can serve as shelves. If the café is self-service provide a till and a checkout, suitably labelled and with 'ch' highlighted. Write labels for the foods, too, along with prices. Special offers advertising delights such as 'Try chocolate for children!' will help extend vocabulary as well as provide a focus for words containing 'ch'.

If you have room for an extended role play area, you could include two small plastic tables and chairs. Children's garden furniture is ideal and reasonably priced. A menu can be written on card to stand up on each table in booklet format. Highlight all the 'ch' digraphs in another colour.

A menu list can be displayed on the café wall, too. Use toy foods, salt dough models or, for an opening event, have real party food for everyone. Foods could include choose, chips, chocolate, cherries, cherry pop, chapattis, chick peas, chicken and cheesecake.

Salt dough is made by mixing plain flour and salt in a ratio of 2 flour to 1 salt measure. Add 1 teaspoon of cooking oil and mix with water to a malleable consistency. Treat it as pastry and mould whatever shapes are required. Bake them very slowly in a cool oven until hard but not brown. When they are cold, paint them and coat them with varnish when dry.

Have a brainstorming session with the children to think up new food descriptions for the menu, for example, chilly chips, chapatti chips, cheese chips, chocolate chips and cherry chips; chopped cherries, chopped chapattis and chopped chillies; cheesy chops, choccy chops and cherry chops; chocolate chums and cheese chasers.

Consonant Digraph th

The digraph 'th' can be found in the initial, medial or final position in a word. It has two sounds which are only slightly different in the way they are pronounced. First, there is the 'tongued th' as in 'these', 'those' and 'they', and second the 'blown th' as in 'think', 'thick', 'thank', 'both' and 'bath'.

Real Things

Introduce the digraph with a display of actual objects that start with 'th', such as a Thermos, a thread, a theme park (ticket or brochure), a thermometer, a 'thank you' card, a thistle and a thimble. Include at least one item in which 'th' is at the end of the word, such 'teeth'.

Create a corner display for the items by cutting the corner off a cardboard box and covering the box with coloured paper. The drop-shadow letters 'th' in the title are made by cutting out two of each letter in different colours and positioning one slightly lower than its twin. Let the children attempt to cut out their own 'th' from card, with or without a drop shadow as you see fit. Using a thick black pen, draw 't' and 'h' about 10 centimetres high. Photocopy several and encourage the children to cut out and glue the letters to a coloured card of their choice.

Traffic Lights

This can be used for identification of the three digraphs or to display word lists for each in a lift-the-flap format.

To make a lift-the-flap traffic light display, cut six white circles to the same size as each coloured paper circle and glue three onto the black card. Glue the remaining white circles to the reverse sides of the coloured paper circles. Using adhesive tape to make hinges, attach the tops of the coloured circles to the tops of the white circles. Write eight words for each digraph as shown in the photograph, so that children can lift the flaps and read the words.

Table Activities

The following easy activities will draw attention to many words that start with 'th'.

Thick and Thin

Label two trays 'thick' and 'thin'. Provide a number of thick and thin items such as thick and thin books, pens, rolls of tape, fabrics and threads. The children must sort the items and place them in the correct tray.

Writing

Provide a small blackboard and some coloured chalks and ask the children to practise writing the digraph in different colours. If necessary, stick a small adhesive label in the corner of the board to show how the digraph is written.

Counting 3, 13 and 30

You will need no fewer than 50 construction bricks and a board to attach them to. Cover one side of three large bricks with cards labelled: 'three 3', 'thirteen 13' and 'thirty 30'. The children must put 3 bricks on the board and place the correct label alongside, and continue in the same way, counting and labelling 13 and 30 bricks.

Thank you, thank you, thank you!

Let the children make 'thank you' cards which they can send to anyone they want to thank. Look at commercial designs on used cards and cut out appropriate pictures. Glue the pictures (or their own illustrations) onto a folded sheet of white card and decorate with glitter. Encourage the children to trace or copy the words 'thank you' from a card or off the board or to trace over your writing, according to their ability. Ask if anyone can remember how to spell the words without looking.

Thelma and Theo

This is a list showing the two pronunciations of 'th' for the children to use as reference when they are writing and learning to spell the words from memory.

Draw a cartoon-style girl and boy on a large sheet of white paper. Give both a striped T-shirt and show one character with their tongue sticking out. Between the stripes on this character, write a list of 'tongued th' words. On the other, write a list of 'blown th' words. Label the characters 'Thelma' and 'Theo'. Cut decorative edges down the sides of the card and glue them onto a larger sheet of red card, also cut to create a border. These lists can include commonly used parts of speech, such as 'this', 'those', 'these', 'they', 'them', 'then', 'the' and 'thin', 'thick', 'thank' and 'three'.

Make a Word

These devices can be used by individuals to make and copy a word list. Use card rectangles about 18 by 10 centimetres and write four or five word rimes on each card and draw a box about 2.5 centimetres square to hold the onset of each. (On each card, list rimes that will make words using the same 'th' sound – either tongued or blown.) To make the moveable onset, cut a strip of card 2.5 by 5 centimetres and write 'th' on the far right in colour. Attach this to the word card with a 20 centimetre length of wool.

To use the card, the child places the onset 'th' over a square to complete a word. Children can read out the words to the class, a group or a partner, or copy them onto paper.

Critical Features

When children recognise whole words it may be that they quickly take in the shape, size, length and, possibly, the initial letter. As they become more experienced as readers and listeners, they also begin to use contextual cues to identify new words. To help them to recognise these critical features and develop a strategy for both reading and writing, spend some time examining them in frequently used words or new vocabulary you encounter.

3D Words

This focuses on the shape of words, enabling children to make words with shapes.

You will need a selection of double- and single-sized construction bricks. Turn them onto their sides so that the joining notches all face right and completely cover the top facing sides with self-adhesive labels. Decide which words you are going to use and write out the letters as shown with ascenders and descenders on double bricks and small letters on single bricks. Include a coloured baseline and a different coloured mid-line on all of them. Make up the letters you need and make a shaped flash card for each word for the children to use to match and make the words.

Cut-out Words

This device emphasises the baseline of writing and shows the position of ascenders and descenders. Look at their position in the words, count how many there are in each word and identify the letters' names and sounds if appropriate.

Choose six to ten words that you want to study, such as high-frequency words or c-v-c words with the same rime. Cut out all the letters that are needed from a sheet of thick, coloured paper. Then cut a strip of paper in another colour that is as wide as the standard letter 'a' and as long as you need for all the words to go on the line with spaces inbetween. Stick the words on the coloured paper strip and display it against a wall or a paper background so that the ascenders and descenders stand out.

The paper strip can also be used to gather words of a certain type (words with ascenders, descenders, no ascenders, and so on).

Capital Letters and Names

Use a class session to discover the variety of different capital letters that are used in the children's names. See if anyone can spot that all capitals are ascenders. To focus on this, write their names on a sheet of white paper and draw round the shape. Use a variety of colours to fill in the area around the shape.

Variation

Organise high-frequency words into changeable lists using flash cards. They can be sorted into
- words with ascenders
- words with descenders
- words with no ascenders or descenders
- words with both
- alphabetical order
- words with one, two, three, four and five letters.

Display the high-frequency words in alphabetical order to introduce the idea of a dictionary.

Bouncers

Once you have introduced features like the consonant digraphs 'th', 'ch' and 'sh', and blends such as 'bl' and 'st', encourage the children to spot these features in new words.

Make some touchable bouncing labels on which to write letter partners as a focus. Cut out circles of coloured card and write a blend on each. Cut strips, 2 by 10 centimetres in size, from a plastic drinks bottle. Use adhesive tape to attach one end of each strip to a 'sound circle' and staple the other end to a display board. Children usually enjoy looking at activities like this with a friend and get useful language exposure at the same time.

For a fun activity, mount several bouncers as shown and ask one child to touch a bouncer of their choice. The rest of the group must think of two or three words starting with this sound and make a silly name or phrase, for example 'Sheena shines sheep', 'slip, slap slop', 'blue blinkers'.

Familiar Words

We use the written word for many different purposes: to name things, to greet, warn, direct, persuade, reward, comfort, organise, control and entertain. It's a tall order for children to learn all this at once but we can start by developing a rich reading environment around them and by using the written word to help us direct the events during the day. This requires the display of labels, lists, posters, information and rewards. It is also important to make their use obvious, for example, 'I'll just read my special list with children's names on it' or 'This sign tells us to wait quietly'.

Signs and Labels

The class name plate, children's coat peg labels and labels for trays and cupboards containing general resources will all need to be in place when school starts. To help classify items and places and to help children recognise names and colours, use a colour code for the background paper of labels, for example yellow for tray labels, blue for the coat pegs, orange for art things.

Label everyday objects, such as chairs, doors, windows and the floor, as well as children's toys, such as bikes and building bricks. Use cut-out catalogue pictures of the toy or equipment to stick onto the label to provide a visual clue. Make labels and signs for different areas in your classroom or work base, and use related shapes as shown in the photograph. If possible, redo labels in new colours during a year so that the children's attention is refocused.

Staff Photographs

To help the children learn the names of school staff through conversation and to begin to read those familiar names, display a set of named photographs of the staff (a shaped poster as shown can be eyecatching). Position the display at a level suitable for children to point to and read easily.

Reading Book Characters

If you use a reading scheme, the names and personalities of the characters will be familiar to the children. To aid recognition of these names, display them on an open book for the children to browse through.

Cut a large piece of thick white paper into two and fold each piece in half to produce double-page shapes. Cut out pictures of the characters and stick either several pictures of the same character on a single page, or one large image of the character, and name them. Staple the back and front pages to the wall and then staple the centre-fold of the second piece so that it can be turned like a book.

Variation

Take time to focus the children's attention on the words around them by playing some of the following games:

- I Spy – 'I spy a word that starts with b/f/g' (the word must be somewhere on the walls)
- Close Eyes – ask individuals to close their eyes and spell out the sounds of a c-v-c word that is displayed on the wall

- Invisible Writing – turn to the board and pretend to write a two- or three-letter word (from the high-frequency word list) in clear letters and ask the children to guess the word by concentrating on the shape of the letters
- Give Us a Clue – using clear actions, mime an appropriate word from a topic or a list on the wall (e.g. run, sit, cat). Ask the child who guesses the word to point to it on the wall.

Word Flags

Pop a 'word flag' in the pencil pot on each table so that the children can learn to read a small selection of familiar words from current texts or themes, for example: 'Goldilocks', 'bears', 'father' or 'spring', 'grow', 'baby'.

Use a thick plastic straw and a 10 centimetre square of coloured paper to make each flag. Fix the paper to the end of the straw with adhesive tape. Write two or three words on each side of the flag. Put different words on each table or repeat a small selection. Make a collection of about 50 flags so that the flags can be moved and replaced regularly.

Common Words

There are certain common words in English that appear with great frequency (see page 71). They are short, and some have irregular spellings, but they play an important grammatical part in even simple texts for new readers. Children must acquire these as sight vocabulary in order to progress as new readers. They can be learned through a combination of activities, both in the context of a sentence and on their own.

Table-top Lists

Select six high-frequency words on which to focus, using current sentence work and current handwriting practice of letter groups as a basis for your choice. Write four duplicate lists, each in a different colour, and make a set of these four lists for each writing table. Stick the lists onto the table with sticky-backed plastic, in a cross formation, leaving the centre free for a pencil pot.

The children can refer to these lists as they write. Change the words as necessary.

Lotto

Prepare four 'lotto' cards in different colours for each game you make. Mark out the cards, as shown in the photograph, and write the same six high-frequency words on each. Write the same words on four white sheets of card of the same size.

Cut them into separate word cards so that you have four sets of each of the words found on the coloured card. These word cards can be put into a tin with a top hand-hole or into a drawstring bag, so that the children can't see which one they are picking.

To play the game, in groups of four, give each child a coloured lotto card and put the bag or box of words in the middle. Show the children how to take turns to dip into the bag and pick a word that they can then match with one on their card. They then cover the coloured space with the white word card. If a child picks a word they have already covered, the word should go back in the bag. The child with all the words on their lotto board covered is the winner.

Twizzlers

Cut thick white paper into an 8 by 16 centimetre rectangle. Fold the rectangle once into a square and write a different high-frequency word on each side of the square. Open out the rectangle and use adhesive tape to attach the end of a drinking straw to the back of one of the squares. Fold the rectangle over and fix it down with a roll of adhesive tape. Make about six twizzlers in this way.

Use them by holding the straw between your palms and rotating it from side to side so that you turn the words into view. Use them to play, 'Which word now?' The children can 'twizzle' the words to friends and ask them to read them.

I'm a Word Fan!

Concertina-fold a sheet of paper into about eight strips. Halfway along, write four to eight high-frequency words, one on each fold. The words can be tailored to suit individual needs. Encourage the children to write the words alongside or underneath yours – if they are doing this with an adult helper the words will be constantly read and spoken. Help the children to decorate any remaining sections and add patterns along the edges. Write a child's name on each if appropriate. Once decorated, help the children to fold the paper into a fan by gathering the folds together at the base and fixing with adhesive tape.

Use the fans as a novel and fun 3D word list. Let the children take them home to read to the family.

Word Kids

This is another novel type of word list presenting high-frequency words in groups of six or fewer which can be used for daily reference in the classroom.

Ask the children to draw faces on white paper and to cut them out. Draw simple outlines of body shapes on coloured card and cut them out, too. Attach a face to each body outline. Divide each body horizontally with lines, or fold into concertinas, and write a word in each space. Display these on a wall in a place near to the writing tables. Add more paper children to the line-up, as necessary. Use one 'word kid' for each list of words that start with the same sound.

Walter Word Worms

Cut out strips of paper and divide them into five sections. Leave the left-hand section empty and write a word in the four remaining sections. Children can copy the words from the board. Cut out circles 8 centimetres in diameter from paper and ask the children to decorate these as faces for the worms. Staple or glue these to the left-hand side of the body in the space remaining, then fold the bodies for a 3D effect. The children can write their names on the reverse and take the lists home. Tailor the lists to suit individuals' needs.

Word Wheel

This device will help children to focus on a word they need when writing. Limit the number of words presented to maximise their learning.

Cut out a circle from white card, as shown in the photograph. Segment the circle into six with a pencil and write a word in each section. Be careful to write the word above the section line so that the word will appear straight when viewed through the window. Decorate the outside edge of the circle. Cut out a window from a sheet of coloured card, making sure that the window will reveal a word when the circle is positioned underneath (the circle will have to be positioned so that it sticks out from behind the card at one side). Fix the card over the top of the circle with a brass pin.

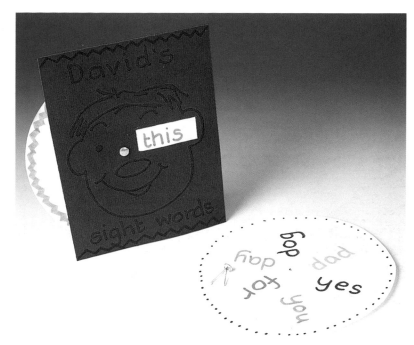

Use this as a mini word bank when doing sentence work, or for a game in which children have to find a certain word.

Sentence Holder

This device helps the children to see words in their proper context as parts of sentences. Coloured card can be folded as shown to make a card holder. Secure both ends with adhesive tape. Cut out squares and strips of card and write one word on each, selecting words that can be used to form short sentences. If you include the children's first names in the cards then the sentences will be more meaningful. Use high-frequency words such as: 'this', 'is', 'a', 'we', 'he', 'she', 'went', 'come', 'was', 'going', 'like'.

Word Holders

Cut out cards to cover the front face of construction bricks and write a selection of words on these. Glue them to the bricks. These can be made into sentences, using a board from a construction kit as the sentence holder.

Special Collections

When you begin short topic work you may be looking at themes such as 'Ourselves', 'Homes', 'Pets' and 'Summer' and you will want to present short vocabulary lists to focus the children's attention on the relevant selection of words and how they are written. Some children may have started to write short statements and sentences and a collection of working words will help them. Present the collections in a form that is visually linked to the subject.

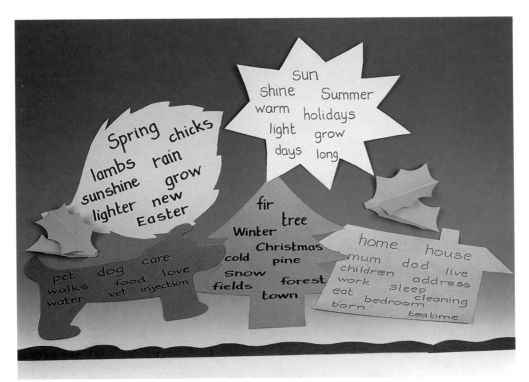

Lists in Shapes

Using any odd pieces of paper, cut out large shapes that are visually linked to the theme and write your list of words on them. For example, cut out a house shape for vocabulary on homes. Display the collection in a place that is convenient for all to see during writing activities. Add to your display of these different shapes and label it, 'Our word collection'.

Word Caterpillar

Put a week's collection of words, or topic-related words, on a word caterpillar. Cut out a caterpillar from coloured paper, including several body sections and pairs of legs. Number the body sections in consecutive order and write a list of words on each one. Then you can refer to 'number 5 on the caterpillar' to help a child find a word.

Variation
Create a similar display using the carriages of a train and engine.

Word Hangings

Cut out shapes, such as hearts, stars or leaves, from thin, coloured card. Make five or six for each hanging so that you only focus on a small collection of words at a time. Write one word on each shape. Staple the shapes in line on an 8 centimetre wide strip of toning coloured crêpe paper or card. Hang these on a display board or from the ceiling. For special topics try to use related shapes such as flowers, suns or large letter shapes. The device can also be used to display class names, favourite book title and story characters (useful as a reference at story time).

Variation

For a hand-held list write the words on a card. Cut out a topic-related shape and glue it at the top of the list. Divide the words by coloured lines to make visual discrimination easier.

Shaped Books

Fold one piece of coloured card and two pieces of white paper in half to make a small booklet. Staple the fold. Cut the booklet into a shape (big, broad shapes are best to minimise tearing, for example a tug boat, a house, a barn, a kennel, an apple, a loaf or a car). Add decorative details to the front page along with names and a title. Help the children to write words you are using in the book for their own reference. The book can be for individual or class use.

Colours

Ask older children to paint a large picture, incorporating large areas in a wide range of colours. Make sure the colours are vibrant so that, when displayed, they catch the eye of the younger children. Write the colour names in black on labels cut to a variety of shapes to add interest. Stick them directly onto the colour blocks or make sure that they clearly point to the relevant colour.

Numbers

Words for numbers make an important collection for the classroom. Use an image that can be repeated in a linear form, such as a row of dancing clowns, rabbits or cats. Alternatively, use a caterpillar or train with carriages. The item should be drawn by older children and then photocopied. Display numerals, words and cumulative amounts as shown.

Pictorial Collections

Ask the children to paint collections of objects, such as things found in a room, found in the garden, types of transport, etc. When the paintings are dry, write labels and attach them so they clearly indicate the relevant object. Alternatively, ask the children to paint individual pictures and then supply photocopied lists of about five suitable words for them to cut out and stick on by themselves.

Use these paintings to provide a collection of vocabulary. Topic-related pictures, such as an ambulance or a nurse, are useful for reference in the role-play area. You can use far more words in a collection because there is a direct visual link as a reading clue. Use unusually shaped labels like arrows and pointing hands to add variety and label each painting with the artist's name.

Variation

Ask the children to paint portraits of themselves or staff which can then be labelled appropriately. Help the children to write the labels and add them to the pictures.

To provide a model for the labelling, draw an outline figure on the board and write the labels on for copying. Restrict the number of labels to about five to ensure the task is reasonable before photocopying the outline figure complete with boxes for labels for the children to fill in. They can then colour the figure themselves.

3D Collections

Use an actual object for the display of a word collection, for example a doll or teddy bear could be used for labels of the parts of the body. Write the words on bright, coloured labels that catch the eye. Cut them into arrow shapes and attach them to the object. Large toy cars, engines, planes or dolls' houses can also provide a visual base for vocabulary.

Days of the Week

Cut an octagon shape from white card or stiff paper and divide it into eight sections with a thick felt-tipped pen. Fill one section with a pattern drawn in coloured felt-tipped pen as a visual start/end point for the list. Write a day of the week in each of the other sections using differently coloured felt-tipped pens. Mount the octagon on a contrasting coloured octagon, using a split pin through the centre. Cut out and stick on a paper arrow or pointing finger that can be used to show which day it is.

Seasons of the Year

Display the seasons by using four sections of coloured paper and bordering it with scenes depicting the seasons. Ask older children to draw the black line images representing each of the seasons and photocopy as many as are required to complete the border.

Variation

Ask children to draw self-portraits on small circles of paper to decorate the edge of the season they were born in. Fill any gaps with coloured circles of paper.

Handwriting

If we can present handwriting as an interesting, useful and valued skill from the beginning, we will be setting a precedent for the future. It is now generally agreed that practising handwriting in conjunction with spelling patterns aids the development of both. So, the best approach is to use phonic patterns and whole words currently in use by the children to practise the skill. Handwriting will become an interesting, fun and useful activity which clearly shows the child his or her progress and achievement.

While you will be teaching handwriting as part of your general work, any of the activities on the following pages can be used to further increase the focus on handwriting.

Handwriting House

Set aside a small corner which you can enclose as a handwriting booth. Refer to it as the 'handwriting house' for the sake of the alliteration. Make it as attractive and cosy as possible for two children to use at a time. The enclosure will make it a little quieter to aid concentration.

Use large sheets of flat or corrugated card to enclose a small table and two chairs or stools. Fix the card to the table or the surrounding display wall with staples or parcel tape. Provide a selection of writing materials:

- assorted thicknesses of pencil
- assorted fine and broad felt-tipped pens
- erasers and pencil sharpeners
- assorted colours and sizes of scrap paper
- containers for pens and paper.

Provide material for activities that can be done with or without an adult:

- name cards to trace
- small tracing books (20 sheets stapled together)
- high-frequency words on cards to trace or copy
- pre-handwriting exercises/patterns to copy.

Handwriting Hanging

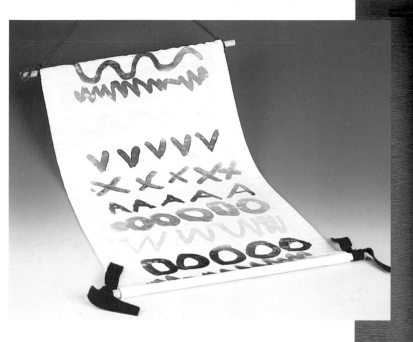

Use fabric paints that can be painted on paper and, when dry, ironed onto fabric.

Use strips of white paper and ask the children to paint symmetrical letters (o, v, l, x, M, T, W, A) and geometric patterns such as zigzags, waves and curls. Iron these onto a long piece of white polyester or cotton fabric in colourful rows. Pattern the rows with felt pens to give further handwriting practice.

Hang the fabric over dowel or thick rolls of art paper. Add a dowel to the bottom of the hanging to weigh it down. Tie cord or thick wool to the top for hanging and additional pieces to the bottom for decoration. Add this to your display.

⚠ **Note:** Children should be well-supervised or kept away from hot irons when used.

Variation
Smaller versions can be made, so that each child completes his or her own 'handwriting hanging'.

Beautiful Butterflies

Cut out a butterfly body shape from coloured card and draw features with a felt-tipped pen. Cut out eight strips of differently coloured paper to fit around the body as wings. Ask individuals to practise rows of letters using fine felt-tipped pens. Glue the end of each strip to the back of the body shape to create wings. Display them in the 'handwriting house'.

Fancy Fish

Draw and cut out fish shapes from white and yellow card. Divide the body of each fish into vertical sections with pencil lines before asking the children to practise writing letters in rows, following the pencil guidelines. Add features to the faces, then cut out thin paper strips from green card to represent pond weed for display, interwoven with the fish.

Name Fans

Concertina-fold coloured sheets of paper. Ask the children to practise writing their name using differently coloured felt-tipped pens between the folds on a sheet. For display, gather the ends of the sheets together and tape them to create a fan. Display others alongside in an open format.

Bright Spark

Cut out a star and comet tail from white and yellow card. Entitle it 'This week's bright spark' and use it to mount an example of good handwriting work each week. Try to make sure that every child's work is displayed at some time.

Letter Bubbles

Create bubble painted prints using various colours of paint. To do this, mix paint with a little water in a plastic container. Then add washing-up liquid and blow into the mixture through a straw. Make several differently coloured mixtures in this way. Place a sheet of paper gently over the bubbles. Carefully lift the paper off to reveal the bubbly print.

Cut out the bubble patterns and add a letter to the centre of each bubble. Each background could be used for a group of letters formed with similar strokes (such as 'o', 'c', 'a', 'd', 'g', 'q'). Cut out blue paper backgrounds, slightly larger than the bubble patterns, to create a blue border. Display the letters and use for reference.

Terrific T-shirts

Cut out T-shirt shapes from white card. Draw pencil lines across to give writing guides. Ask the children to practise letters and regular patterns on these using a variety of coloured felt-tipped pens. Display several T-shirts together in your 'handwriting house'.

⚠ **Note:** Check for any allergies before using detergents.

Drawing Den

Create a 'drawing den' using the same method as for your 'handwriting corner' to create a quiet place to focus on activities. Free drawing acts as 'track training' for handwriting whilst being a wonderful activity in itself to develop the imagination and encourage conversation. Allow only two children at a time into the corner to maintain a quiet atmosphere. In the drawing den supply a variety of pens and crayons in different colours and sizes. Also include different grades of pencil, from hard to soft.

- Supply a variety of paper in different colours, textures and sizes, including very tiny (e.g. 10 centimetre squares) to encourage tightness of line.
- Be ready to supply a subject for drawing if needed, or to stretch any children who always focus on the same subject. Subjects could include: self-portraits, local events, favourite games at playtime, television characters, home, holidays and favourite toys.
- Encourage the children to experiment with different sizes of paper and different drawing media.
- Encourage the children to cover the paper with their work, finish their work and clean up afterwards.
- Ask the children to put their name on their work.
- Mount and display a variety of work to inspire others, including examples of prints by famous artists – both abstract and realistic.

Word, Rhyme and Story Lists

High-frequency Word List

I up look we like and on at for he is said

go you are this going they away play a am cat to

come day the dog big my mum no dad all get in

went was of me she see it yes can

Rhyming Groups

I my

we me he see she

go no

they play away day

come mum

Stories and Rhymes for the Rhyme Room

- Traditional stories with strong rhythm and repetition: *The Gingerbread Man*, *Three Billy Goats Gruff*, *The Little Red Hen*, *Red Riding Hood* and *Henny Penny*.
- Traditional rhymes with strong rhythm, suitable for role-play and actions: 'Baa Baa Black Sheep', 'Old King Cole', 'Hickory Dickory Dock', 'Hickety Pickety My Fine Hen', 'One, Two, Three, Four, Five', 'Jack and Jill' and 'Row, Row, Row the Boat'.
- Counting songs: 'Ten Fat Sausages', 'Five Little Speckled Frogs', 'Five Little Ducks Went Swimming One Day', 'Two Little Dicky Birds', 'Ten Green Bottles', 'Ten in the Bed', 'Five Little Peas'.

For details of further Belair publications,
please write to Libby Masters,
BELAIR PUBLICATIONS LIMITED,
Albert House, Apex Business Centre,
Boscombe Road, Dunstable, LU5 4RL.

For sales and distribution in North America and South America,
INCENTIVE PUBLICATIONS,
3835 Cleghorn Avenue, Nashville, Tn 37215,
USA.

For sales and distribution in Australia,
EDUCATIONAL SUPPLIES PTY LTD,
8 Cross Street, Brookvale, NSW 2100,
Australia.

For sales and distribution (in other territories),
FOLENS PUBLISHERS,
Albert House, Apex Business Centre,
Boscombe Road, Dunstable, LU5 4RL,
United Kingdom.
Email: folens@folens.com